. Publishers (India)
the Bookmaster
DELHI

Language Skills

Pre-Primary Learning Skills
B
Crayon

Early Grammar

Shab

This book belongs to

____

____

AF798538

D. S. Publishers (India)

First Published 2001
22nd Reprint 2022

ISBN 978-81-87131-69-4

Published by
DS Publishers (India)
7/7 Ansari Road, Daryaganj
New Delhi 110 002
+91 11 4156 3757
info@dspublishers.com
www.dspublishers.com

Type-setting and Cover Design by
Lovika Arts

Printed at
Balaji Offset

₹ 135

PREFACE

Children of the ages between 3 years and 5 years are at the Pre-Primary stage of learning, and just about awakened to their sensory skills.

This series of books is basically revolving round children of these ages — and are thus directed towards the development of the skills to which the tiny beings are getting introduced to. They are being initiated into the concepts that are necessary for further progress of the learning procedures.

This set of books deals separately with specific language skills. With these books at hand, followed by the guidance of the teacher or parents will take the children ahead in fixing in their minds the correct concepts necessary for further education.

The activities enshrined in these books help the child in developing his/her basic skills of reading and writing.

Male and Female

ick out the correct word and write it in the box.

man	woman
boy	girl

eacher/Parents : Nouns are names of people, places or things. Nouns are related to Gender (Male/Female).

Male and Female

Give the name to the people in the picture. Write the correct word in each box.

grandfather	father	brother
grandmother	mother	sister

One and Many

Fill in the blanks with the missing words.

one boy

two boys

one dog

three dogs

one cup

four ______________

one bird

many birds

one bee

many ______________

eacher/Parents : Nouns are also related to Numbers (Singular/Plural).

One and Many

Write the missing words.

A big doll

Two small ____________

One ____________

Many ants

One crayon

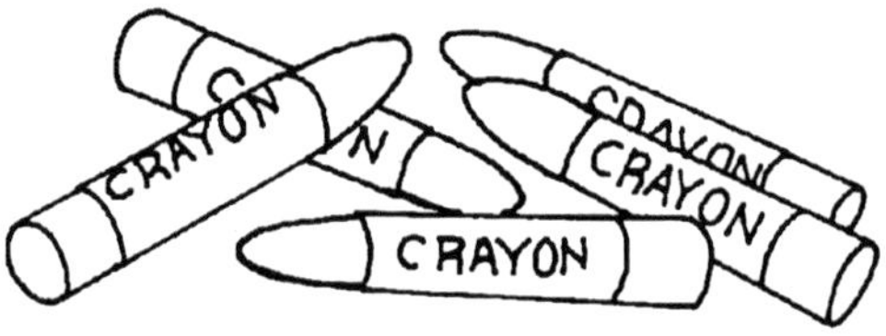

Many ____________

A big fat pig

Three little ____________

A happy ____________

Two happy clowns

Teacher/Parents : Most plurals are formed by adding 's' to singular nouns.

Use of 'I am'

Paste your photograph here.

Tick the correct word in the box.

I am a	boy	girl .

I am a [boy | girl].

I am [four | five | six] years old.

I am [tall | short].

I am [fat | thin].

Teacher/Parents : Ask the child to read the sentences and words in the boxes carefully.

Use of 'I am'

Fill in the blanks with the missing words.

Teacher/Parents : Reinforce the use of 'I am' by adding more sentences, e.g., **I am a student**, **I am fond of chocolates**, etc.

Use of 'I am'

ill in the blanks with the missing words.

I am ; My

Draw or paste the pictures in the frames.
Fill in the blanks with the missing words.

Frame	
Myself	I am a ______________ My name is ______________
My mother	This is <u>my</u> mother. I love my ______________
My father	This is <u>my</u> father. I love ______ ______________ .
My sister	This is <u>my</u> sister. I play with ______ ______________ .

Teacher/Parents : Ask the child to practise the use of 'my' e.g. my bag, my school, my pet, my friend.

Use of 'my'

ll in the blanks.

I have a dog.

This is my dog.

I have a kitten.

This is ______ ______________.

I have a doll.

This is ______ ______________.

I have a top.

This is ______ ______________.

acher/Parents : Ask the child to tell you what body organs belong to him/her.

Use of 'He is'

Fill in the missing words.

This is Gopal.

Gopal is my friend.

He is my friend.

This is John.

John is a student.

He is a student.

This is Mr. Paul.

Mr. Paul ________ a doctor.

________ ________ a doctor.

This is Mr. David.

Mr. David ________ a policeman

________ ________ a policeman

Teacher/Parents : Direct the child, how 'He' replaces male singular noun.

Use of 'He is'

Complete the following sentences.

Use of 'She is'

Fill in the blanks with the missing words.

This is Rani.

Rani is a pretty girl.

She is a pretty girl.

This is Miss Mary.

Miss Mary _is_ a nurse.

She _is_ a nurse.

This is Sheila.

Sheila ____ a tall girl.

________ ____ a tall girl.

This is Mrs. Das.

Mrs. Das ____ a teacher.

________ ____ a teacher.

Teacher/Parents : Direct the child, how 'She' replaces female singular noun?

Use of 'She is'

omplete the sentences with the correct words.

Use of 'He is/She is'

Look at the pictures carefully.
Draw lines to join the words correctly.

He is

She is

a policeman

a teacher

a nurse

a doctor

a postman

Teacher/Parents : Help the child to distinguish 'he' and 'she'.

Use of 'his' and 'her'

in the blanks with the missing words.

This is Peter.

This is Peter's

This is his dog.

This is Mr. Paul.

This is Mr. Paul's

This is his car.

This is Shelly.

This is Shelly's

This is her doll.

This is Mrs. Malik.

This is Mrs. Malik's

This is ____________.

cher/Parents : Encourage the child to speak of my cap, his cap, her cap, your cap.

Use of 'his' and 'her'

Tick ☑ the correct answers.

My brother has a cat.

This is	his	cat.
	her	

My father has a computer.

This is	his	computer.
	her	

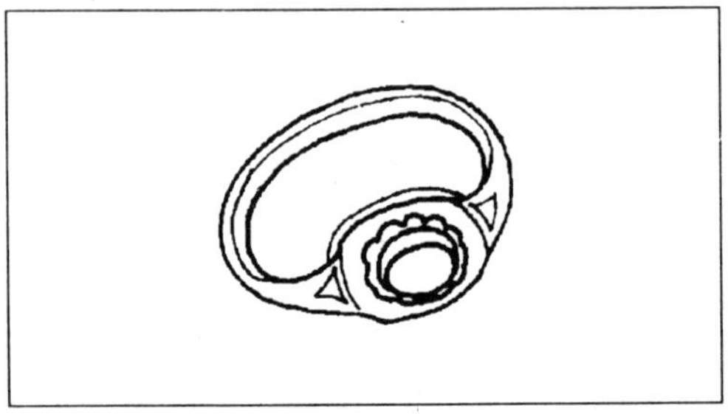

My mother has a ring.

This is	his	ring.
	her	

My friend, Ravi has a bicycle

This is	his	Bicycle.
	her	

My sister has a toy-train.

This is	his	toy-train.
	her	

Use of 'you' and 'your'

ace the words.

You have a rabbit.

Is this your rabbit?

You have a bicycle.

Is this your bicycle?

Is this your pen?

cher/Parents : Keep on asking the child "Is this your................. ".

Use of 'my', 'your', 'his' and 'her'

Fill in the blanks with my, your, his and her.

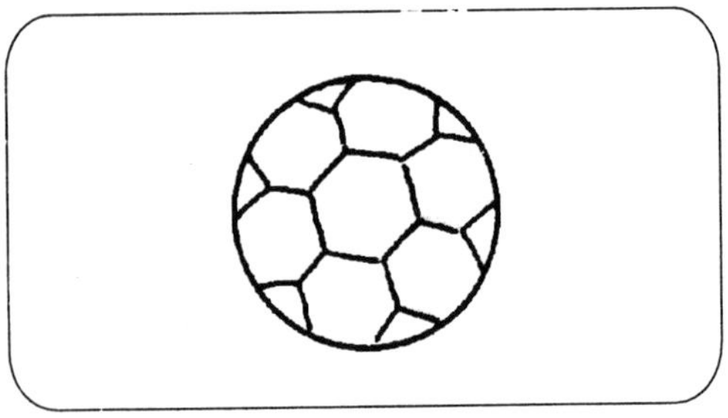

He has a ball.

This is __________ ball.

I have a parrot.

This is __________ parrot.

You have a hen.

This is __________ hen.

She has a watch.

This is __________ watch.

He has a bicycle.

This is __________ bicycle.

Use of 'We are'

ace and copy the sentences.

I am studying.

I am studying ______ .

Mona is studying.

______ .

Mona and I are studying.

______ .

We are studying.

______ .

acher/Parents : Introduce the concept of 'We'.

Use of 'We'

Tick☑ the correct sentence.

☐ I am playing.

☐ He is playing.

☐ She is playing.

☐ He is playing.

☐ We are playing.

☐ You are playing.

Use of 'We'

Look at these pictures carefully. Complete the sentences.

I am singing.

I am singing.

My mother is singing.

My mother is singing.

My father is singing.

My father is singing.

______ are singing.

'Happy Birthday' to Granny.

Use of 'They are'

Complete the sentences.

Two girls are dancing.

They are dancing on the stage.

Ali and Gopal are walking.

They are walking to school.

The ox and the bull are fighting.

________ ______ fighting in the field.

Three dogs are running.

________ _____ running after the cat.

Teacher/Parents : Ask the child to replace plural nouns by the pronoun 'they'.

Use of 'They are'

Fill in the blanks with the missing words.

They are cricket players.

__________ ________ thieves.

__________ ________ doctors.

Revision Exercise

Circle the correct words.

1. My father is reading.

He	is reading a newspaper.
She	

2. My mother is busy.

He	is busy baking a cake.
She	

3. My sister is laughing.

He	is laughing at the clown.
She	

4. My brother and I are going out.

We	are going to the picnic.
They	

5. Grandma and grandpa are in the Living Room.

We	are watching television.
They	

Teacher/Parents : More practice will help the child to differentiate the pronouns like 'he', 'she', 'we', 'they'.

Use of 'am', 'is' and 'are'

Tick ☑ the correct word in each sentence.

She [is / are] a doctor.

He [is / are] my father.

We [is / are] students.

I [am / is] a joker.

They [am / are] soldiers.

Teacher/Parents : Explain the child that a singular subject takes 'is' while a plural subject takes 'are' except 'I' and 'you' which take 'am' and 'are' respectively.

Use of 'is' and 'are'

Fill in the blanks with 'is' or 'are'.

The big fat dog __is__ sleeping.

Two little dogs __are__ barking.

My notebook ________ on the table.

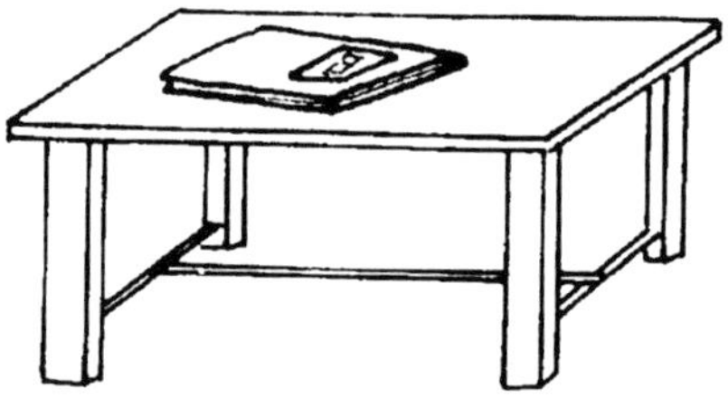

My story books ________ lying on the floor.

One cow ________ going away.

Two cows ________ grazing in the field.

Use of 'is' and 'are'

Fill in the blanks with 'is' or 'are'.

One kitten __________ out of the basket.

Two kittens __________ in the basket.

All the eggs __________ in the tray.

One egg __________ broken.

All the birds __________ flying away.

Only one bird __________ sitting in the tree.

Teacher/Parents : More practice helps the child to distinguish the difference between 'is' and 'are'.

Use of 'do' and 'do not'

Fill in the blanks with 'Yes, I do' or 'No, I do not'.

Do you play football?

Yes, I do ______________________________ .

Do you play chess?

No, I do not ______________________________ .

Do you eat apple?

______________________________ .

Do you eat watermelon?

______________________________ .

____

Teacher/Parents : For further practice ask more questions like 'Do you go to library? or 'Do you watch Cartoon Network?, etc.

Use of 'does' and 'does not'

l in the blanks with 'he/she does' or 'he/she does not'.

oes he watch television?

es, ______ __________ .

oes she watch television?

o, ______ __________ __________.

oes he like reading?

o, ______ __________ __________.

oes she like reading?

es, ______ __________.

acher/Parents : Direct the child to use 'does' with singular pronouns except I and you.

Use of 'do' and 'does'

Fill in the blanks with 'do' or 'does'.

Does the little dog bark?

Yes, it <u>**does**</u>.

Do dogs play?

Yes, they <u>**do**</u>.

Does the black bird fly?

Yes, it ________ .

Do birds fly?

Yes, they ________ .

Does the little duck swim?

Yes, it ________ .

Do ducks swim?

Yes, they ________ .

Teacher/Parents : Provide more examples to strengthen the knowledge of use of 'do' and 'does'.

Use of 'This is'

Look at the pictures carefully. Fill in the blanks.

a tortoise

This is a tortoise.

a ball

This is ______________________ .

This is ______________________ .   my puppy

a clown

This is ______________________ .

Teacher/Parents : Encourage the child with the use of "This is ...." by pointing at various nearby objects.

Use of 'This is'

Complete the sentences.

What is this?

This is a book.

What is this?

__________ ________ a flower.

What is this?

__________ ________ a horse.

What is this?

__________ ________ a hat.

Use of 'This is'

Choose the correct answer by putting a tick ☑ in the box given below.

Is this a dog?

☐ This is a dog.

☐ This is not a dog.

Is this a duck?

☐ This is a duck.

☐ This is not a duck.

Is this a kettle?

☐ This is a kettle.

☐ This is not a kettle.

Is this a car?

☐ This is a car.

☐ This is not a car.

Use of 'That is'

Look at the pictures carefully. Fill in the blanks.

What is that?

a star

That is a star.

What is that?

a snake

That is ________________ .

a bird

What is that?

That is ________________ .

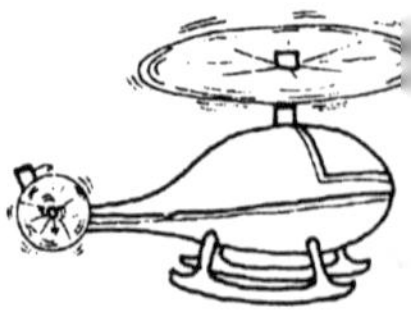

What is that?

a helicopter

That is ________________ .

Teacher/Parents : Ask the child 'What is that?' by pointing at the far-away objects.

Use of 'That is'

omplete the sentences.

That is a kite.

__________ ________ a giant.

__________ ________ a car.

__________ ________ a rocket.

eacher/Parents : Encourage the child with the use of "That is a ...."

Use of 'These are'

Trace and fill in the blanks with correct words.

These are cows.

The cows are grazing in the field.

These are dogs.

The ________ are barking at the thief.

These are apples.

The ________ are delicious.

________ are ducks.

The ________ are swimming in the poc

Teacher/Parents : 'These' is the plural of 'this'.

Use of 'This' and 'These'

Draw lines to match the pictures with the correct sentences.

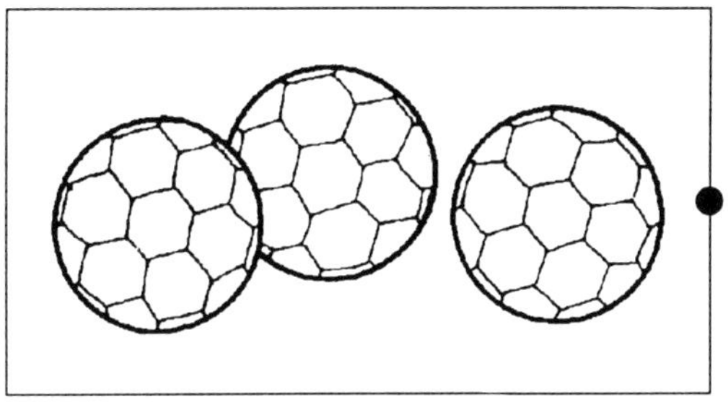

• This is a teddy-bear.

• These are pears.

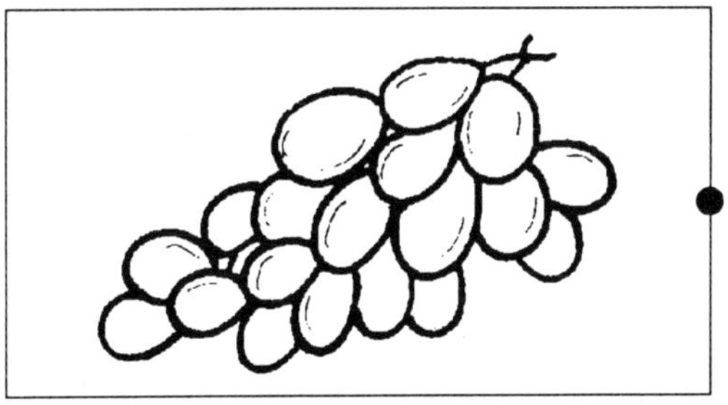

• These are balls.

• This is watermelon.

• These are grapes.

Teacher/Parents : Ask the child for more practice for correct use of 'This is' and 'These are'.

Use of 'Those are'

Complete the sentences.

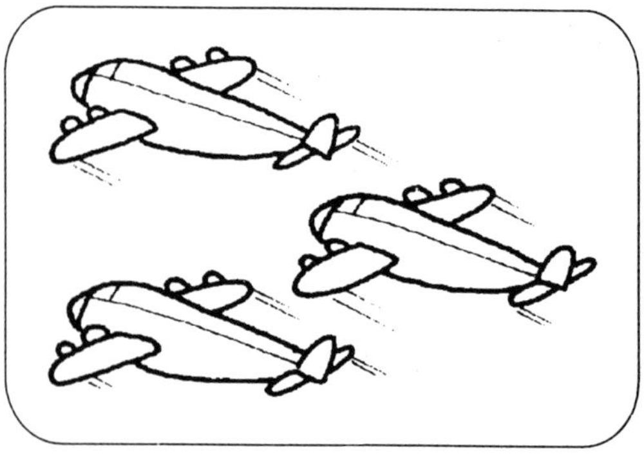

Those are aeroplanes.

The __________ are flying in the sky.

Those are birds.

The __________ are flying away.

Those are bees.

The __________ are flying away.

Those are cars.

The __________ are running up the hill.

Teacher/Parents : 'Those' is the plural of 'that'. 'Those' points at the far away objects.

Use of 'That' and 'Those'

Draw lines to match the pictures with the correct sentences.

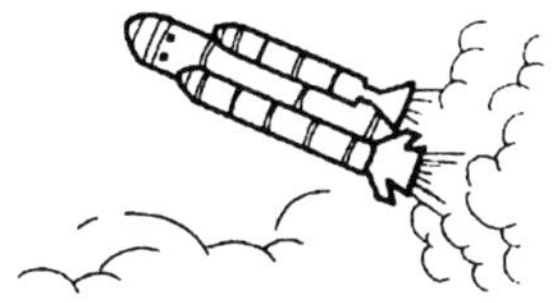

• Those are balloons.

• That is a rocket.

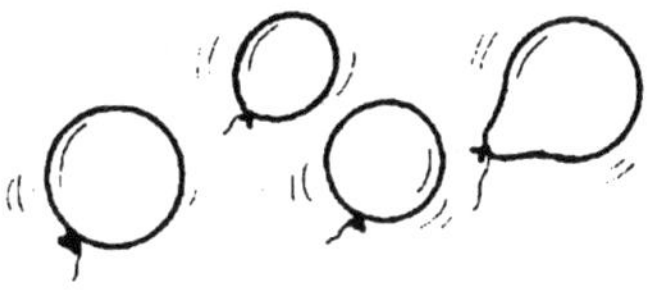

• Those are birds.

• Those are butterflies

• That is a bus.

Teacher/Parents : 'That is' for singular noun.
'Those are' for plural noun.

Use of 'I have'

Colour the toys you have.

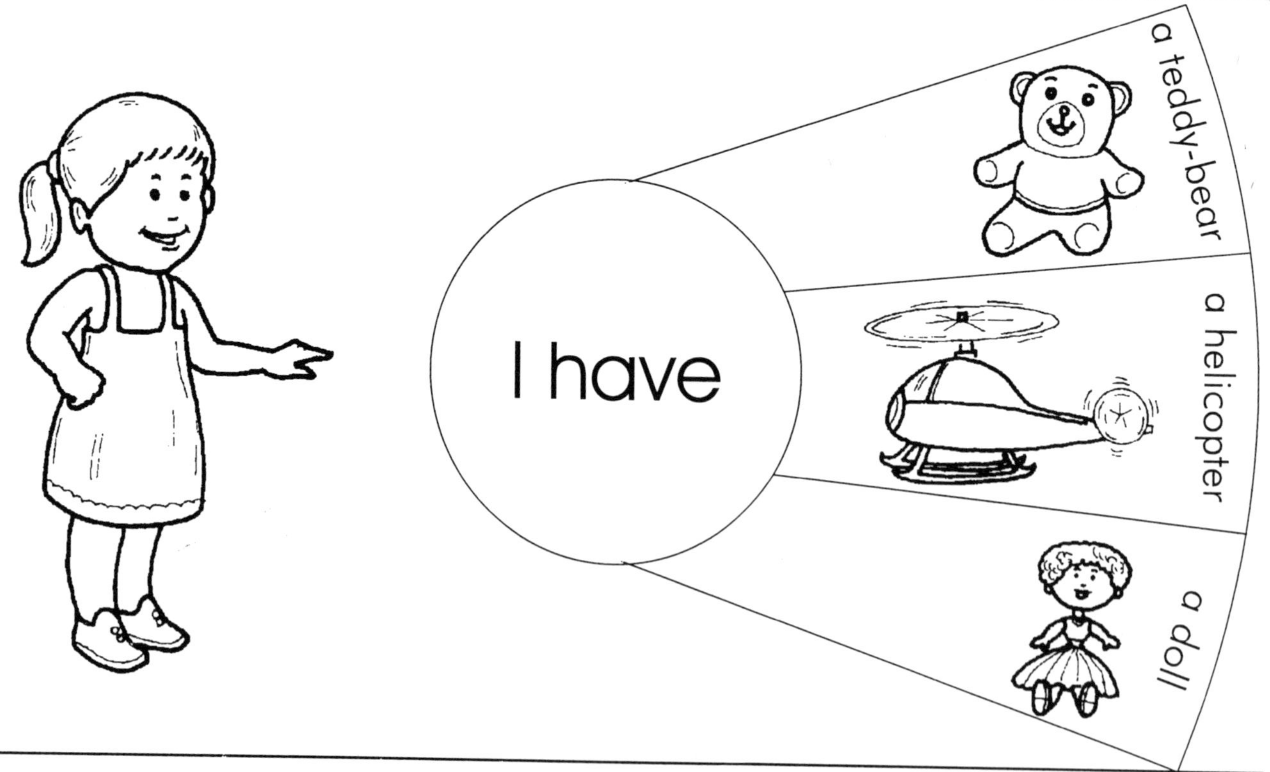

Teacher/Parents : Encourage the children to tell you, 'What they have' in their school bags, etc.

Use of 'I have'

What do you have ? Fill in the missing words.

nose

I have one ________ .

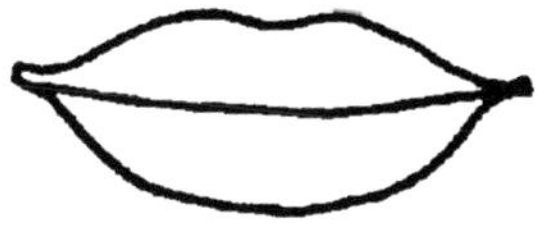

mouth

I ________ ________ ________ .

ears

I have two ________ .

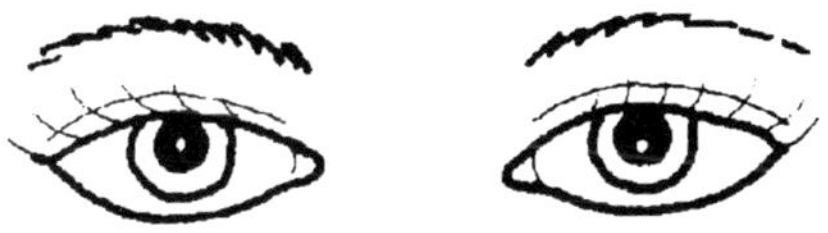

eyes

I ________ ________ ________ .

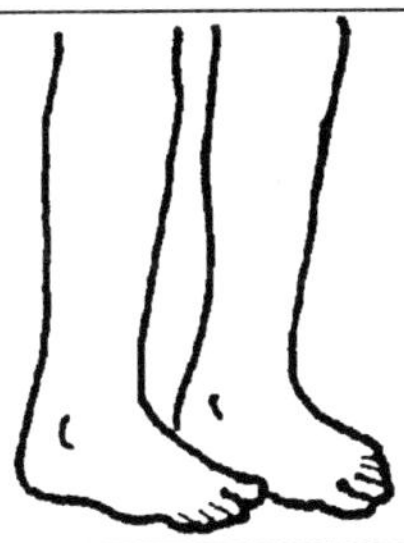

legs

I ________ ________ ________

Use of 'I have'

Choose the correct sentence and put a tick ☑ in the box.

This is my dog.

I am a dog. ☐

I have a dog. ☐

This is my bicycle.

I am a bicycle. ☐

I have a bicycle. ☐

This is my toy-train.

I have a toy-train. ☐

I am a toy-train. ☐

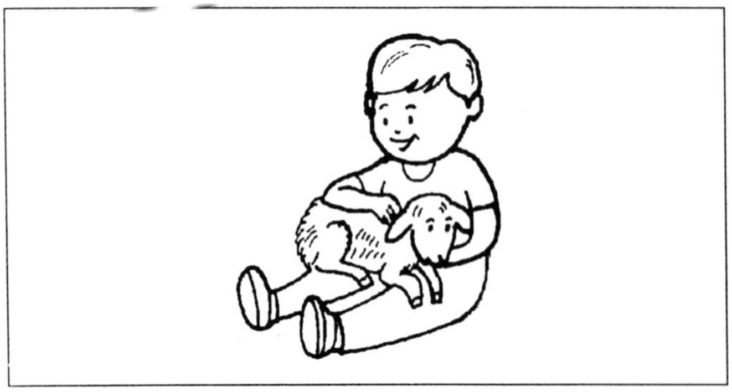

This is my lamb.

I am a lamb. ☐

I have a lamb. ☐

Teacher/Parents : Ask questions like 'What do you have in your room?', 'What do you have in your pocket?' etc. for more practice on the use of 'I have'.

Use of 'He has'

Fill in the missing words and complete the sentences.

This is Gopal.
Gopal has many pets in his house.

cow
dog
kittens
parrot
rabbit

Gopal has two kittens.

He has a ______________________

He ______________________

He ______________________

He ______________________

Teacher/Parents : The use of 'He has' may further be practised by asking the name of the things that Father/Grandfather/Uncle has.

Use of 'She has'

Look at the pictures carefully and complete the sentences.

This is Julie.
Julie has many things in her room.

dolls
teddy-bear
bicycle
aeroplane
story book

Julie has two dolls.

She has a ______________________

She ______________________

She ______________________

She ______________________

____

Teacher/Parents : Further practice on the use of 'She has' may be done by asking about the things that Sister/Mother/Aunt has.

Use of 'They have'

ook at the room of Peter and John carefully.
Vhat do they have in their room?

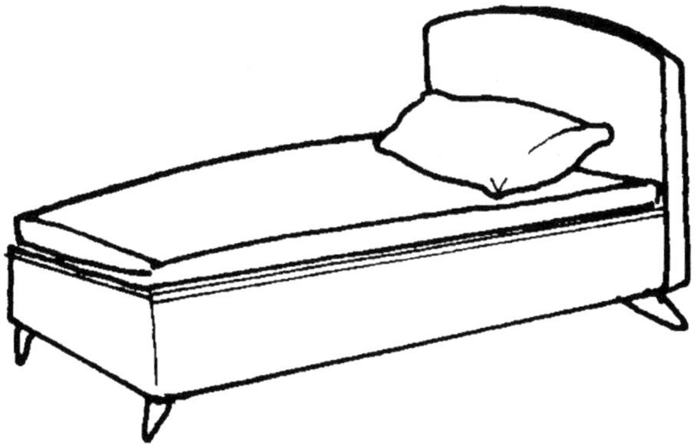

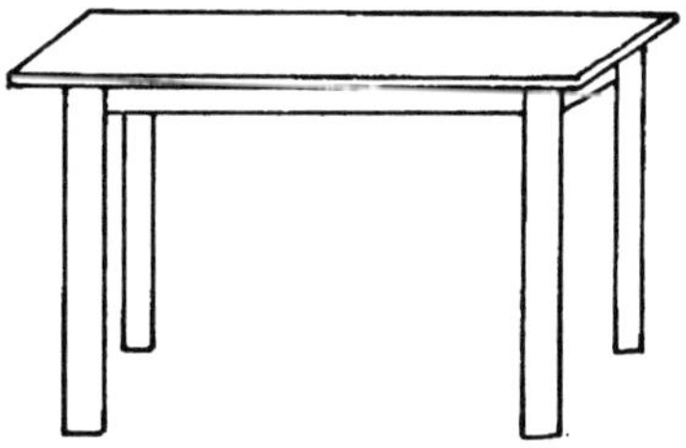

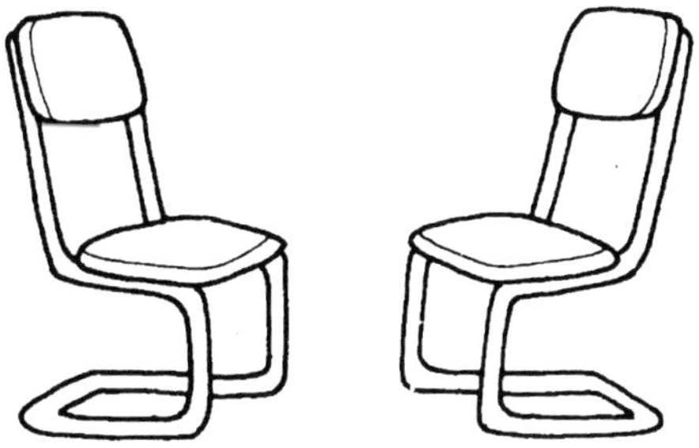

ɔed
ɔhairs
ables
ɔomputer
oy-train

ᑭeter and John have a <u>bed</u> .

They have

They have

They

They

eacher/Parents : Ask the children to look at their neighbours and 'What do they have?'.

Use of 'We have'

What do you all have at your home?
Complete the sentences.

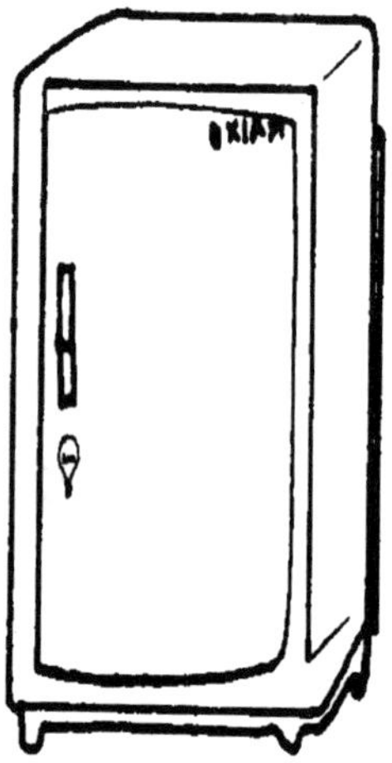

television-set
sofa-set
oven
refrigerator
telephone

We have a television-set.

We have

We

We

We

Teacher/Parents : Assist the child to list the things that he/she and his/her parents have at home. Ask him/her to practise writing 'We have ....

Use of 'It has'

ll in the blanks with the correct words.

ook at the elephant.
· has long ears.

t ________ a ________________ .

.ook at the eagle.
t has wings.

t ________ sharp ________________ .

.ook at the fish.
It has scales on its body.

It ________ two ________________ .

Use of 'has' and 'have'

Look at the picture.
Tick ☑ the correct sentence.

Tony has a balloon.

☐ He has a balloon.
☐ She has a balloon.

Mary has a toy car.

☐ He has a toy car.
☐ She has a toy car.

Lily has a vase.

☐ She has a vase.
☐ They have a vase.

Gopal and Ali have a ball.

☐ He has a ball.
☐ They have a ball.

Use of 'He and She', 'has and have', 'his and her'

Circle the correct words.

My father has / have a car.

He / She has a beautiful car.

This is his / her car.

My mother has / have a hen.

He / She has a fat hen.

This is his / her hen.

Use of 'and'

Fill in the blanks with 'and'.

Ravi

Karim

Ravi <u>and</u> Karim

Dolly

Rita

Dolly ________ Rita

cup

plate

cup ________ plate

cow

calf

cow ________ calf

Teacher/Parents : 'And' is a linking word (conjunction). It is used to connect two or more nouns.

Use of 'and'

Draw lines to match the pictures with the correct words.

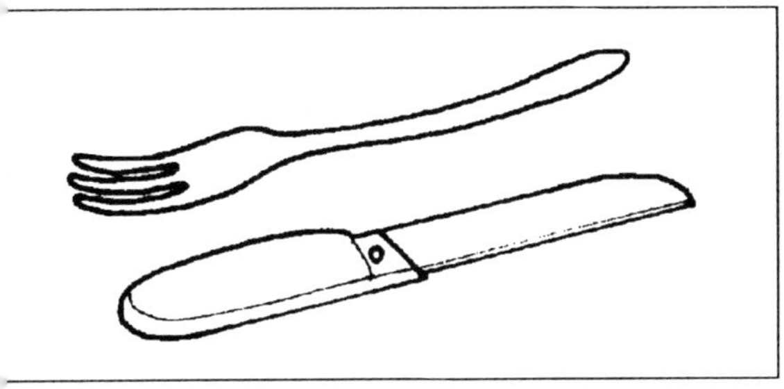

moon **and** stars

bus **and** car

knife **and** fork

bat **and** ball

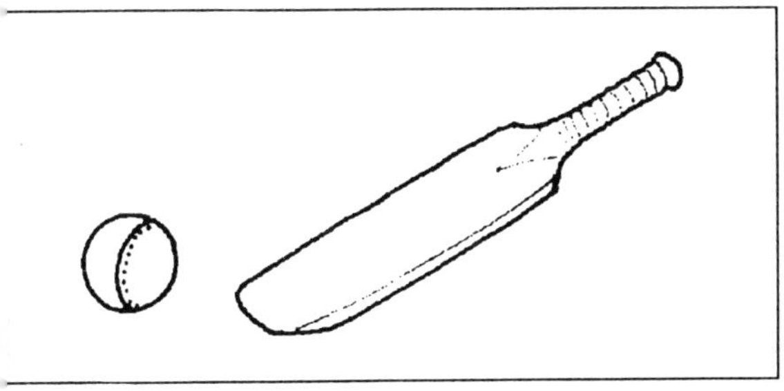

boys **and** girls

Use of 'a' and 'an'

Tick ☑ the correct answer.

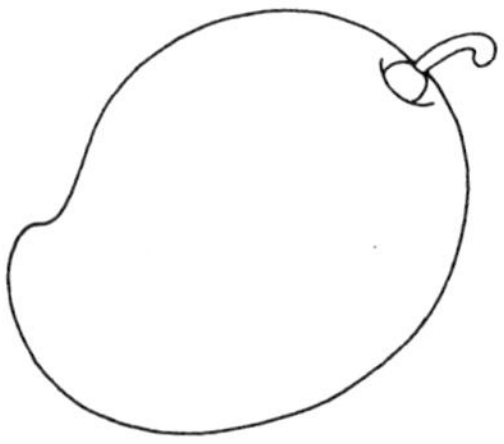

☐ a mango

☐ an orange

☐ a bat

☐ an eagle

☐ a lion

☐ an elephant

☐ a stick

☐ an umbrella

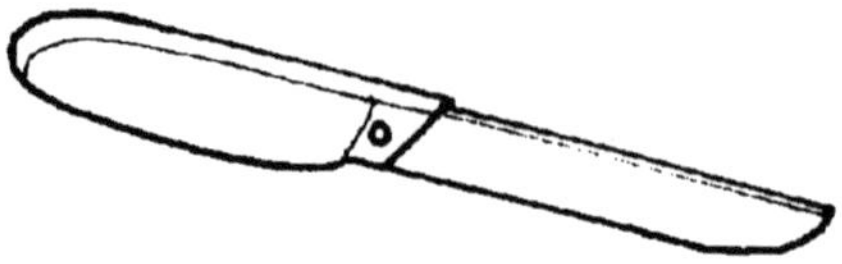

☐ a knife

☐ an axe

Teacher/Parents : Direct the child to use 'an' for words beginning with vowel sounds of a, e, i, o and u.

Use of 'a' and 'an'

Read and trace the words.

This is a pear.

This is an apple.

This is a lion.

This is an elephant.

This is a pen.

This is an inkpot.

This is a parrot.

This is an owl.

Use of I can/cannot

Tick ☑ the correct answer.

Can you see?

Yes, I can see.
No, I cannot see.

Can you play football?

Yes, I can play football.
No, I cannot play football.

Can you read?

Yes, I can read.
No, I cannot read.

Teacher/Parents : Read the questions to the child. Use 'I can' to show the ability to do task and 'I cannot' to denote the unability.

Use of 'she can/cannot'

What can Granny do? Fill in the missing words.

Can Granny knit?

Yes, Granny can knit.

Can Granny sew?

Yes, Granny can sew.

Can she bake a cake?

Yes, she ______ ________ a cake.

Can she drive?

No, she cannot drive.

Can she run?

No, she __________ __________.

Use of 'he can/cannot'

What can Grandpa do? Fill in the blanks with the correct words.

Can Grandpa run?

Yes, Grandpa can run.

Can Grandpa read?

Yes, Grandpa can read.

Can he play?

Yes, he __________ __________.

Can he drive?

Yes, he __________ __________.

Can he cook?

No, he __________ __________.

Use of 'We/They can/cannot'

Fill in the blanks with 'can' or 'cannot'.

Ravi and Ali are friends.

They can climb.

The girls are in kitchen.

They ________ cook.

My brother and I are players.

We ________ ________ football.

Sheila and I are neighbours.

We ________ sew together.

Use of 'can' and 'cannot'

Fill in the blanks with 'can' or 'cannot'.

Simmy is a little girl.

She ______________ swim.

John is a smart boy.

He ______________ cycle.

Gopal and Karim are little boys.

They ______________ play football.

Tina and I are singers.

We ______________ sing well.

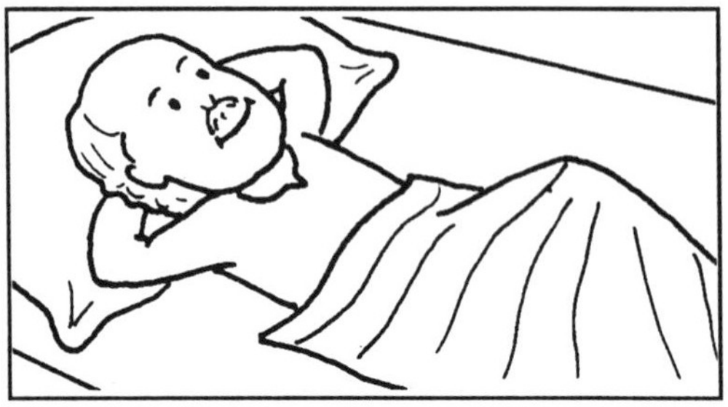

Mr. Paul is too weak.

He ______________ walk.

Sentence Structure

Rearrange the words in puzzles to make a sentence.
Write the sentence on the line.

He toys many has

is That pen her

are friends They good

cannot A read baby

a is This book

Sentence structure

Rearrange the jumbled words to make a sentence.
Write the sentence on the line.

I
brush
my teeth
can

____

____

is
a
pen
This

____

____

are
a smart
You
boy

____

____

a
have
television
We

____

____

swim
cannot
I

____

____